Understanding Marketing

Pocket Mentor Series

The *Pocket Mentor* Series offers immediate solutions to common challenges managers face on the job every day. Each book in the series is packed with handy tools, self-tests, and real-life examples to help you identify your strengths and weaknesses and hone critical skills. Whether you're at your desk, in a meeting, or on the road, these portable guides enable you to tackle the daily demands of your work with greater speed, savvy, and effectiveness.

Books in the series:

Understanding Marketing

Expert Solutions to Everyday Challenges

Property of
Baker College of
Allen Park

Harvard Business Press

Boston, Massachusetts

Copyright 2010 Harvard Business School Publishing

All rights reserved

Printed in the United States of America

14 13 12 11 10   5 4 3 2 1

Library of Congress Cataloging-in-Publication Data

Understanding marketing : expert solutions to everyday challenges.

p. cm. — (Pocket mentor)

Includes bibliographical references.

ISBN 978-1-4221-2892-3 (pbk. : alk. paper)   1. Marketing.

HF5415.U264 2009

658.8—dc22

2009032262

Contents

New Offerings: A Potent Marketing Tool   59

Suggestions for creating fresh products and services to market.

Putting Your Marketing Plan into Action   65

Ideas for working with your marketing department and the marketing process to ensure success.

Spotlight on Direct Marketing   71

A focused look at this special form of marketing.

Spotlight on Relationship Marketing   83

A closer examination of this special form of marketing.

Tips and Tools

Tools for Understanding Marketing   93

Worksheets to help you calculate the lifetime value of a customer, determine how customers quantify the value of your offerings, conduct a SWOT analysis, create a product profile, and draft a marketing plan.

Test Yourself   103

A helpful review of concepts presented in this guide. Take it before and after you've read the guide, to see how much you've learned.

Key Terms   111

Frequently Asked Questions   117

To Learn More   121

Further titles of articles and books if you want to go more deeply into the topic.

Sources for Understanding Marketing   131

Notes   133

For you to use as ideas come to mind.

Mentors' Message: Why Understanding Marketing Is Important

No matter where you work in your organization or what your job responsibilities are, it's vital that you understand marketing. That's because marketing is all about understanding and delighting customers—and without customers, an organization can't exist. Anyone can contribute insights about customers to other managers, executives, and project leaders in their company and thus sharpen the firm's marketing efforts.

This book helps you make a contribution by covering the fundamentals of marketing—including how marketing relates to a company's mission, how marketing to consumers differs from marketing to organizations, ways to understand your company's competitors, how to develop a marketing strategy and marketing communications plan, tactics for creating new products and services, ways to ensure that your marketing plan is effectively executed, and how to use direct marketing and relationship marketing effectively.

Marketing is a big subject; thus, this book covers a lot of ground. But by familiarizing yourself with the basic concepts and tools provided here, you'll be well positioned to help your company get the most business value from its marketing efforts.

Philip Kotler, Mentor

Philip Kotler, the S.C. Johnson & Son Distinguished Professor of International Marketing at Northwestern University's Kellogg School of Management, is a world-renowned expert on strategic marketing. Philip's research spans a broad number of areas, including consumer marketing, business marketing, services marketing, and e-marketing. He has authored over forty-five books, including the best-selling *Marketing Management* (Prentice Hall, 2009, 13th ed.), *A Framework for Marketing Management* (Prentice Hall, 2009, 4th ed.), *Principles of Marketing* (Prentice Hall, 2010, 13th ed.), and *Marketing Moves* (Harvard Business School Press, 2002). In addition to teaching, he has been a consultant to IBM, Bank of America, Merck, General Electric, Honeywell, and many other companies. He also has received over twelve honorary degrees from around the world.

Bruce Wrenn, Mentor

Bruce Wrenn, the William E. Colson Professor of Marketing at Andrews University, has served as a consultant to organizations in the high-tech, packaged-food, fine dining, health care, pharmaceutical, and biotech industries, as well as to not-for-profit organizations. He has authored more than a dozen books in marketing management and planning, marketing research, church marketing, and consumer behavior. He has served as a Harvard ManageMentor since 2002.

Understanding Marketing: The Basics

What Is Marketing?

What's the first thing you think of when you hear the word *marketing*? Do you imagine salespeople talking up their company's products with potential customers? Flashy billboard ads lining a highway? Finance managers calculating the possible profits that a new product may bring in?

If you envisioned any or all of these things, you're on the right track: selling, advertising, and profitability calculations are all important parts of marketing. But marketing consists of so much more.

In the pages that follow, we'll examine a definition of marketing, explore how marketing connects with an organization's mission, see how a marketing orientation works and how it connects to customers' needs, examine several approaches to marketing, and review the marketing process.

A definition

The following is a comprehensive definition of marketing:

MARKETING is the process of planning and executing the conception, pricing, promotion, and distribution of ideas, goods, and services to create exchanges that satisfy individuals' and companies' goals.

Marketing isn't somebody's responsibility—[it's] everyone's responsibility.

—Jack Welch

Marketing and mission: A close connection

Marketing starts with the organization's mission, which answers the following questions:

- How does the organization define itself ?

- What are its goals?

- Who are its customers?

- How does it intend to fulfill its mission?

- What is the company's very reason for existence?

For example, "Company ABC's mission is to provide low-pollution cars at a price that customers consider affordable and to foster its employees' and shareholders' achievement of their personal objectives."

Fulfilling an organization's mission is the process of reaching its goals through the exchange of goods, services, and ideas. And it's these activities that define the process of marketing.

Marketing orientation

Effective marketing in any organization requires what's called a marketing orientation. A marketing orientation occurs when *everyone* in the organization is constantly aware of:

- Who the company's customers are

- What the company's customers want or need

- How the firm can satisfy those customer needs better than its rivals can

- How the firm can satisfy customer needs in a way that generates the kind of profits the company wants to achieve

Marketing orientation begins at the top level of planning and requires an understanding of the company's mission as well as its strategy—the concrete actions the company must take to achieve its mission. For instance, to fulfill its mission of providing low-pollution cars at a price that customers consider affordable and fostering its employees' and shareholders' achievement of their personal objectives, a company must define a strategy that involves mastering the latest vehicle-emissions technology. (See "Tips for Building a Marketing Orientation" for additional information.)

Tips for Building a Marketing Orientation

- **Persuade all employees of the need to be customer-focused.** Show employees that the best thing they can do for the company and themselves is to constantly think of new ways to satisfy the firm's most profitable customers.
- **Design the right rewards.** Ensure that your group's performance-measurement and reward systems encourage behavior that builds long-term customer satisfaction.
- **Hire strong marketing talent.** Hire and retain people with substantial marketing experience and skills.

- **Suggest—or develop—in-house marketing-training programs.** Such programs will highlight the importance of a marketing orientation to your firm.
- **Support efforts to restructure the company as a market-centered organization.** The end result—a truly companywide marketing orientation—will position your firm for vital new achievements.

In a company that has a marketing orientation, everyone views marketing as a companywide enterprise, understands the company's mission and strategy, and is familiar with basic marketing principles. This is true whether a person is:

- A product manager or marketing professional in a large corporation

- A production manager who directs the creation of the product

- Someone who's starting up a new business

- An employee of a not-for-profit or educational institution

- A member of a small, growing company

Whatever *your* work situation, familiarity with marketing basics can help you adopt a marketing orientation and thereby contribute to your company's success.

The first step in adopting a marketing orientation starts with understanding customers.

Connection to customer needs

Marketing is a way of understanding and satisfying the customer. Once you understand your customer's (or target market's) basic drives, you can set about satisfying their:

- **Needs.** These are fundamental requirements, such as food, air, water, clothing, and shelter. Beyond the purely physical requirements, people also need recreation, education, entertainment, and a place within a community or social status.

- **Wants.** These are needs that are directed at specific objects that might satisfy those needs. For instance, you might *need* food, but for a special occasion you may *want* to have a meal at a restaurant rather than preparing your food at home.

- **Demands.** These arise when people both want a specific product *and* are willing and able to pay for it. Demands can take several forms. For instance, "latent demand" is when customers have a strong need that can't be satisfied by existing offerings, and "irregular demand" is when demand varies by season, day, or hour.

Marketing is the whole business seen from the customer's point of view.

—Peter Drucker

Marketing focuses primarily on customer needs, since they are the underlying force for making purchasing decisions. These needs can be further broken down as follows:

- **Stated needs**—what customers *say* they want; for example, "I need a sealant for my window panes for the winter."

- **Real needs** what customers *actually* require; for example, a house that is better insulated and therefore warmer during the winter.

- **Unstated needs**—requirements that customers don't happen to mention, for example, an easy solution to insulating the house.

- **Delight needs**—the desire for luxuries, as compared to real needs.

- **Secret needs**—needs that customers feel reluctant to admit; for example, some people may have a strong need for social status but feel uncomfortable about admitting that status is important to them.

Having a marketing orientation helps you determine what type of need is driving a customer's demand. For instance, if a salesperson in a hardware store responds only to a customer's *stated* need ("I need a sealant for my window panes") and does not attempt to discover the customer's *real* need ("My house needs to be better insulated for the winter"), the salesperson might miss a great opportunity to tell the customer about her store's high-tech insulation services and begin to develop a relationship with that customer.

Once an organization begins to successfully meet customers' needs and even exceed their expectations, customer satisfaction rises. Loyalty follows, bringing with it a significant and measurable impact on the bottom line.

How to fulfill customers' needs? Successful companies adapt their offerings to match those needs. Offerings can take numerous forms. Here are some examples:

- **Goods**—physical offerings such as food, commodities, clothing, housing, appliances, and so forth

- **Services**—such as airline travel, hotels, maintenance and repair, and professional expertise (from accountants, lawyers, engineers, doctors, and so on)

- **Experiences**—for example, a fun visit to a theme park or a luxurious dinner at the most popular restaurant

- **Events**—for instance, the Olympics, trade shows, sports, and artistic performances

- **Persons**—such as artists, musicians, rock bands, celebrity CEOs, and other high-profile individuals

- **Places**—cities, states, regions, and nations that attract tourists, businesses, and new residents

- **Properties**—including real estate and financial property in the form of stocks and bonds

- **Organizations**—entire companies (including not-for-profit institutions) that have strong, favorable images in the public's mind

- **Information**—produced, packaged, and distributed by schools, publishers, Web-site creators, and other marketers

- **Ideas**—concepts such as "Donate blood" or "Buy savings bonds" that reflect a deeply held value or social need

Any organization that engages in developing and offering one or more of these "products" to customers is engaged in marketing.

Approaches to marketing

Your company can achieve its mission by satisfying customers' needs, wants, and demands through the products it offers. But how exactly does your organization accomplish this task? By deciding what *kind* of marketing orientation to adopt. The table "Marketing Orientations" shows examples of how the type of marketing orientation a company adopts is driven by particular beliefs and influences what the company focuses on.

All five of the marketing orientations shown in the table have merit. Indeed, each one builds on the one preceding it but emphasizes something different. For example, if your company emphasizes societal marketing, that doesn't mean it ignores the importance of efficient production, high-quality products, selling, or obtaining knowledge of customers. It means that it adds a new dimension—social and ethical concerns—to its marketing approach.

Some companies may even change from one orientation to another in order to stay competitive. To illustrate, many companies—including popular health-and-beauty-product manufacturers and ice-cream makers—have achieved impressive profits by emphasizing

TABLE 1

Marketing orientations

Marketing orientation	The belief behind it	Company focus
Production	Consumers prefer products that are widely available and inexpensive.	High production efficiency, low costs, and mass distribution of products
Product	Consumers favor products that offer the most quality, performance, or innovative features.	The design and constant improvement of superior products, with little input from customers
Selling	A company has to sell its products aggressively, because consumers won't buy enough of them on their own.	Using a battery of selling and promotional tools to coax consumers into buying, especially unsought goods (such as insurance or cemetery plots)
Marketing	The key to achieving a company's goals is its ability to be more effective than its rivals in creating, delivering, and communicating value to its target customers.	Target markets, customer needs, coordination of all company functions from the target customer's point of view
Societal marketing	A company's task is to determine its target customers' needs, wants, and interests—and to satisfy them better than their rivals do, but in ways that preserve or enhance customers' and society's well-being.	Building social and ethical considerations into marketing practices; balancing profits, consumer satisfaction, and public interest

societal marketing. That's because more and more consumers are demanding products that are kind to human communities and the environment.

The marketing process

Within an organization, the marketing process begins at the strategic planning level and then moves to the planning and implementation stages in each area of the company. The process consists of these steps:

1. **Analyze market opportunities.** Identify target customers, understand their needs, and know your competition.

2. **Develop a marketing strategy.** Brainstorm new product ideas, define their competitive edge (that is, the main reasons customers should buy your products instead of your competitors'), and test-market your ideas.

3. **Create a marketing plan.** Decide how you'll position, price, and promote a product, which distribution channels you'll use, and so forth.

4. **Put your marketing strategy and plan into action.** Prepare for surprises and disappointments and incorporate feedback and controls into the implementation process.

5. **Evaluate the effectiveness of your marketing strategy and plan, and adjust them accordingly.** Whatever your position is in your organization, your awareness of the marketing process and participation in it will help your company achieve its marketing and strategic objectives.

In the sections that follow, we'll explore these steps in greater detail. But let's turn now to the first step in the marketing process: identifying the market opportunities that will best help your company achieve its mission, given the products and services that the company has to offer.

To determine these opportunities, you must answer two questions:

- *Who* are your target customers?

- *Why* should they buy your product and not your competitors'?

Your firm probably has many different potential customers who may be interested in your company's offerings. But they likely fall into one of two main categories: individual consumers or businesses and organizations.

Whether your firm sells mainly to individual consumers or businesses depends on its mission. For example, if your company makes electronic gadgets for the home, you probably sell primarily to individual consumers. But if your firm makes high-speed photocopy machines or offers management consulting or corporate financial services, you probably sell to businesses or organizations.

On the other hand, your company's primary market may shift over time if such a change would have strategic value. To illustrate, an automobile manufacturer that sells mainly to individuals might see some advantages in developing and marketing certain kinds of vehicles—such as limousines—for business customers.

In the next sections, we'll look first at ways to market to consumers and then at ways to market to businesses.

When Your Company Markets to Consumers

I f your company markets to consumers, it's vital to understand the forces affecting consumer buying, the process that consumers go through when they're buying, and the strategies that can help you deepen your understanding of consumers.

Forces affecting consumer buying

Understanding the forces that affect consumers' buying behavior helps you identify the most appropriate offering to fulfill your target customers' demands. The truth is that people decide to buy products and services for many different reasons. The table "What Affects Consumer Buying?" shows just a few examples of the forces—cultural, social, personal, and psychological—that most influence individuals' purchasing decisions.

The buying process

In addition to being influenced by a range of forces in their buying behaviors, consumers go through a fairly predictable series of steps when they decide whether to buy something. You've probably followed these steps many times:

1. **Recognize a need**—for example, your computer has become outdated, and you need a new one.

TABLE 2

What affects consumer buying?

Cultural forces	National values, such as an emphasis on material comfort, youthfulness, or patriotism	Ethnic or religious messages or priorities	Identification with a particular socioeconomic class
Social forces	Friends, neighbors, coworkers, and other groups with whom people interact frequently and informally	Family members, friends, parents, spouses, partners, children, siblings	Individuals' own status within their families, clubs, or other organizations
Personal forces	Age, including stage in the life cycle; for example, adolescence or retirement	Occupation, economic circumstances, and lifestyle (or activities, interests, and opinions)	Personality and self-image, including how people view themselves and how they think others view them
Psychological forces	Motives, conscious and subconscious needs that are pressing enough to drive a person to take action; for example, the need for safety or self-esteem	Perceptions (interpretations of a situation), beliefs, and attitudes (a person's enduring evaluation of a thing or idea)	Learning, changes in someone's behavior because of experience or study

2. **Search for more information**—such as surfing the Internet for details on the various features offered by computer companies.

3. **Weigh the alternatives**—"That computer seems to have more memory than this other one."

What Would YOU Do?

"It's Not *My* Job. (Or Is It?)"

JANET SCHEDULED a meeting with Dan, the head of accounting, to talk about her latest market research. Her studies indicated that customers found their monthly billing statements confusing. Dan didn't see what the problem was—customers were paying their bills and his department was keeping track of the money. What more did accounting have to do? Janet asked if Dan's group could develop clearer statements that would make customers' own accounting easier. She said that these sorts of issues were all part of marketing and maintaining the company's mission of delivering products to customers that were easy to use and affordable. Dan was baffled. Weren't the marketing and product development folks in charge of that stuff? Why did he and his group have to worry about these issues?

What would YOU do? The mentors will suggest a solution in *What You COULD Do.*

---

4. **Decide to buy**—you determine that the price is right, conclude that you've done enough "shopping around," and buy the product.

5. **Evaluate and act on the purchase**—you may feel satisfied, disappointed, or even delighted with your purchase; you may

return the product or decide to buy it again; you may use and dispose of the product in ways that are important for marketers to know.

When marketing to consumers, it is also important to think about what your target customers value. Review your own experiences as a customer: How do you determine what's most important to you? Did you get the results you expected? Were the results delivered the way you wanted them? Was the price what you were hoping for?

Strategies for conducting consumer research

A key element in marketing to consumers is conducting research into your target market's needs and preferences. How do you do this? Here are a few ideas:

- Review your company's *internal sales and order information*—which reveal existing customers' buying patterns and characteristics.

- Gather *marketing intelligence*—which you collect through reading newspapers and trade publications; talking with customers, suppliers, and distributors; checking Internet sources; and meeting with company managers.

- Perform *market research*—which is conducted by either an internal research department or an outside firm through devices such as market surveys, product-preference tests, focus groups, and so forth. (See "Steps for Market Research" for more information.)

- Use *secondary data sources*—such as government publications, business information, and commercial data.

By studying the forces that influence consumers' decisions—as well as the process that consumers go through in deciding whether to buy—you can figure out how best to reach and serve these customers.

Steps for Market Research

1. **Define the marketing opportunity you will focus on.** Create a specific question about a marketing opportunity that you want to explore. For example, suppose you work for an automobile maker and your supervisor wants to explore the potential benefits of providing global positioning system (GPS) navigation devices in its cars. You might ask this specific question: "Will offering such a device create enough incremental preference and profit for our company to justify its cost against other possible investments?"

2. **Establish your research objectives in exploring the opportunity you identified.** Decide what kinds of information you'll need to gather to evaluate the market opportunity. Again, asking the right questions can lead you to a clearer understanding of your research objectives.

   For example, a series of questions will help you prepare your market-research plan. In this case, you might ask:
   - "In what way would GPS add value for our customers?"
   - "What kinds of customers would be most likely to use such a device?"

- "How large might the target market be?"
- "What are our competitors offering?"
- "What share of the target market could we expect to gain?"
- "How might different price points affect the sales of cars with the device?"
- "How will offering this device affect our brand image?"
- "How important is a GPS device relative to offering other kinds of improvements to our product, such as safety features?"

3. **Develop your market-research plan.** Make decisions on the following market-research aspects:

- **Data sources.** You can gather *primary* data (gathered for a specific purpose or project) or *secondary* data (collected for another purpose and already existing somewhere, such as a prospect database).
- **Research categories and techniques.** You can choose among various research tools, but be careful to choose the most effective technique to fulfill your objectives.
  - Qualitative research, such as focus groups (bringing potential customers together to talk about the concept)
  - Quantitative research, such as surveys (mail, telephone, online, and so on) intended to count or measure
  - Causal research, such as test-marketing the GPS at different price levels
- **Research instruments.** Select from questionnaires or mechanical devices; for example, an infrared eye-tracking system can reveal how consumers view GPS screens (where their glance lands first, how long it lingers, and so on).

- **Sampling plan.** Decide whom you'll contact as research respondents, how many, and how you'll choose them.
- **Customer-contact methods.** Choices include mail, telephone, personal contact, or online interviews. Each method has its advantages and disadvantages. For instance, mailed questionnaires usually generate low or slow response rates but may help you reach people who normally would not feel comfortable giving personal interviews.

4. **Implement your market-research plan.** Collecting the information can be both rewarding and frustrating. Prepare to run into some of these problems:
   - Respondents who aren't home must be recontacted or replaced.
   - Some respondents won't cooperate as you had hoped.
   - Some respondents may give biased or dishonest answers because they feel pressure to provide opinions or viewpoints that they think you want to receive.
   - Some interviewers may be biased or dishonest in the way they deliver the questions to respondents, because they themselves are hoping to receive particular opinions or viewpoints from potential customers.

   By being aware of these problems and being willing to analyze data with a critical eye, you can help reduce the likelihood or potential bias of these problems.

5. **Analyze the information.** Tabulate the data you gathered, and then apply various statistical techniques and decision models to analyze the results. Marketing-decision-support systems—coordinated collections of data, systems, tools, techniques, and software—can help. These resources may include

statistical tools such as multiple regression and conjoint analysis, game theory, and heuristics.

6. **Present your findings.** Present the major findings that are relevant to making the key marketing decisions facing you or your company. For example, your report may be as brief and cogent as the following statements:

   - "Drivers mainly envision using in-car GPS devices during emergencies, specifically, if they get lost."
   - "In the United States, about thirty drivers in a hundred would buy a GPS device as an in-car option if the device cost $300. About fifteen in a hundred would buy one if the device cost $400. Thus, pricing the device at $300 would yield more revenue ($9,000) than pricing it at $400 ($6,000)."
   - "An international market in areas where maps are not as readily available as in the United States presents our greatest opportunity for GPS."

What You COULD Do.

Remember Dan's bafflement about being asked to deal with marketing issues?

Here's what the mentors suggest:

What Dan needs to realize is that everyone in a company, from product developers to accounting staff, needs to understand the basics of marketing so that he or she can contribute to the effort of bringing value to customers. Dan should review Janet's research and understand exactly what customers find confusing about their statements. He should identify what customers want in a statement and explore ways to redesign the form to better meet customers' needs. By taking this customer-centric approach, Dan would be upholding his company's mission of clearly communicating with customers and creating high-quality products. In turn, he would be adopting what's referred to as a "marketing orientation."

When Your Company Markets to Organizations

Does your company market to organizations instead of to individual consumers? If so, you'll need to learn about the various types of organizations, the forces affecting organizations' buying behavior, and the process that organizations go through when they're deciding whether to purchase a product or service.

Types of organizations

When organizations rather than individual consumers buy from your company, the whole marketing picture changes. Why? Organizations differ from individual consumers in important ways. For one thing, they buy goods and services in order to produce their *own* offerings—which they then sell, rent, or supply in some other way to other customers. Thus, they're usually looking for the best possible deal for their company as a whole.

Organizations can also take many different forms. But these forms fall into three main categories—each of which has different characteristics. The table "Types of Organizations" shows examples.

Forces affecting organizational buying

Organizations are influenced by a different mix of forces than individuals are in their buying decisions. The table "What Influences Organizational Buying?" shows a few examples.

Clearly, marketing to organizations requires very different strategies than marketing to individuals does.

TABLE 3

Types of organizations

Category	Examples	Characteristics
For-profit	Major industries such as manufacturing, construction, communications, banking, services, distribution, and so forth	• Demand for your company's products may change radically in response to just small changes in your business customer's consumer demand. • You work with a smaller number of more professional buyers. • Buyers tend to be concentrated geographically.
Institutions	Schools, hospitals, prisons, nursing homes, and other organizations that provide goods and services to people in their care	• Many institutions have low budgets and "captive clientele." • Your firm might have to package its offerings differently—for example, lower prices, less elaborate packaging—to attract and keep institutional business.
Government	Federal, state, and municipal agencies	• Government organizations typically require suppliers to submit bids. • Public agencies often have complex, time-consuming, purchasing procedures.

The buying process

Organizations also differ from consumers in their buying process. For one thing, they engage in different patterns of buying. Here are some examples of these patterns:

- **The straight rebuy.** The organization regularly reorders office supplies, bulk chemicals, or other materials. If the company buys from your firm, you'll probably feel pressure to maintain the quality of your product.

TABLE 4

What influences organizational buying?

Environmental forces	Interest rates, materials shortages, technological and political developments
Organizational forces	Purchasing policies and procedures, company structures and systems (for example, long-term contracts)
Interpersonal forces	Purchasing staff members' differing interests, authority levels, ways of interacting with one another
Individual forces	An individual buyer's age, income, education, job position, attitudes toward risk
Cultural forces	Attitudes and practices influencing the way people like to do business; for example, Asians tend to emphasize the collective, not individual, benefits of doing business

- **The modified rebuy.** The organization wants to change purchasing terms, such as product specifications, prices, or delivery requirements. If the company buys from your firm, you may feel some pressure to protect the account to keep rivals from encroaching on your business.

- **The new task.** The organization buys a product for the first time, which may require a lengthy and complex decision process between your firm and the company.

On the other hand, businesses go through similar processes that individual consumers go through when making purchasing (procurement) decisions:

1. Recognize a need or problem. For example, "The company's computer system is outdated."

2. Determine the needed item's general characteristics and required quantity—"We need links to all the company's offices."

3. Determine the needed item's technical specifications.

4. Search for potential suppliers.

5. Solicit bids or proposals from suppliers.

6. Choose a supplier.

7. Negotiate the final order—including specifying delivery and installation schedule, final quantity, payment terms, and other details.

8. Assess the chosen supplier's performance and decide whether to maintain the business relationship.

By understanding how the procurement process works, you can design a more effective strategy for reaching and serving business customers.

Understanding Your Competition

Your organization will not be the only one looking at marketing opportunities—whether they lie in marketing to consumers or organizations. Competitors will be looking at these opportunities as well.

The hard fact for businesses is that consumers and organizations typically have choices when deciding who to buy from—and what to buy. Your company wants its target customers to select *your* offerings over your competitors' offerings. But this isn't easy, because competition is intensifying every year.

How can you make sure that your target customers—whether they're consumers or organizations—keep buying from your firm and not your competitors? Your company has to make it clear to its customers what the benefits of your offerings are. But to do that, you need to identify your competitors and compare them.

Identifying your competitors

A competitive analysis can be performed at several levels of an organization. If you're responsible for only one product of many, you still need to perform this analysis.

The first part of any competitive analysis involves determining who your competition is. Be aware that competitors can take many forms:

- Other players offering products similar to yours

- Entirely new players in your industry

- Companies that make substitutes for your products

Most companies have existing and potential competitors. Existing rivals are openly and visibly competing in the same arena. Potential rivals haven't yet declared themselves as players in your industry.

So how do you identify your firm's main existing and potential competitors? Here's an easy rule: *Competitors are companies that satisfy—or that intend to satisfy—the same customer needs that your firm satisfies.*

For example, a customer buys word-processing software that your company makes. Her *real* need isn't for the software—it's for the ability to write. That need can be satisfied by pencils, pens, typewriters, and any other writing tool that an innovative and wily company can dream up. Thus, your company actually has more competitors than you might think.

Not only does your company have more competitors than you might expect, it may also have numerous *kinds* of competitors. For instance, if your company makes photocopy machines, it satisfies customers' need to duplicate documents. But a firm that offers document-duplicating *services*, not a document-duplicating *product*, can satisfy that need just as well. Thus, that service company will be just as much your competitor as another company that also makes photocopy machines.

Comparing your competitors

Once you've identified your existing and potential competitors, compare them by analyzing the following characteristics:

- **Strategies.** For example, does a particular competitor offer a narrow line of high-priced products with high-level, customized service?

- **Objectives.** What is the competitor seeking in the marketplace? (To maximize profits? Market share? Be a technological leader in the industry?)

- **Strengths and weaknesses.** What "share of market" does the competitor possess? That is, how much of your target market does the company sell to? What "share of mind" does it possess; that is, what percentage of customers name that competitor as the first one that comes to mind? And what "share of heart" does the company possess; in other words, what percentage of customers say they'd prefer to buy from that firm before any other? Note that rivals that claim significant shares of *mind* and *heart* will most likely gain market share and profitability.

- **Ways of doing business.** Most competitors fall into one of these categories in terms of how they respond to changes in the marketplace: (1) *slow-moving*—the rival company doesn't react quickly or strongly to other players' moves, perhaps because it feels confident that its customers are loyal, it just hasn't noticed that the game has changed, or it simply lacks the resources to make a move; (2) *selective*—the company responds to certain kinds of attacks, such as price cuts or advertising campaigns; (3) *a "tiger"*—the firm reacts swiftly and strongly to any assault; (4) *unpredictable*—the firm shows no predictable reactions to marketplace changes. How does each of *your* company's competitors do business?

By understanding *all* these characteristics of your competitors, you can design marketing strategies that will increase your chances of coming out on top.

Developing
Your Marketing
Strategy

W hen you've selected your most promising new (or freshly adapted) offering and analyzed your competitors, the next step is to create a marketing strategy.

What is a marketing strategy?

At its heart, a *marketing strategy* answers the question: why should your customers buy *your* product (or service) and not your competitors'? The strategy will later form the heart of your marketing plan for a particular offering.

Marketing strategy happens at several different levels within an organization. In big companies, people create strategy at the corporate level, the SBU (strategic business unit) level, and the product level.

In many smaller companies, strategy creation may take place on all three levels simultaneously. In fact, a product manager developing a market strategy at a small firm might ask not only, "How should we market this product?" but also, "Should we be offering this product at all?"

Next, we look at strategies for crafting your marketing strategy, selecting what's called your marketing mix, differentiating your offering, positioning and branding your offering, and adopting marketing strategies tailored to products versus services.

Crafting your strategy

In creating a marketing strategy for a product, your main goals are: (1) to answer the questions, "What's your product's competitive advantage?" or, from the customer's perspective, "What need would this product or service fulfill more effectively than any other similar offering?" and (2) to ensure that the offering does fulfill the customer's expectations, needs, and desires.

To achieve these two goals, you'll need to know your target market's size and typical behavior (its demographic characteristics) as well as the primary benefit of the proposed product *in your customers' minds*. In addition, you will need to:

- Estimate the sales, market share, and profits that the product could generate in its first few years on the market.

- Establish the planned price, distribution strategy (how you'll get the product to customers), and marketing budget for the first year.

- Project the product's long-run sales and profits.

Selecting your marketing mix

One familiar way to think about marketing a product or service is through the *marketing mix*, otherwise known as "the four Ps" of marketing: product, price, place, and promotion.

- **Product** decisions include quality, design, features, brand name, and so on.

- **Price** decisions include price point, list price, discounts, payment period, and so on.

- **Place** decisions include channels of distribution, geographic coverage, and so on.

- **Promotion** decisions include advertising, direct marketing, public relations, and so on.

Your decision on a marketing mix needs to be coherent. For example, if you're marketing a commodity product, you wouldn't want to give it a high list price.

Differentiating your offering

Another approach to defining a marketing strategy is to consider how you might differentiate and position your promising product or service and how you might create a brand for it.

Differentiation is the act of distinguishing your company's offering from competitors' offerings in ways that are meaningful to consumers. You can differentiate products *physically* or through the *services* your company provides in support of the product.

Products' *physical* distinctions include:

- **Form**—size, shape, physical structure, for example, aspirin coating and dosage

- **Features**—such as a word processing software's new text-editing tool

- **Performance quality**—the level at which the product's primary characteristics function

- **Conformance quality**—the degree to which all the units of the product perform equally

- **Durability**—the product's expected operating life under natural or stressful conditions

- **Reliability**—the probability that the product won't malfunction or fail

- **Reparability**—the ease with which the product can be fixed if it malfunctions

- **Style**—the product's look and feel

- **Design**—the way all the previous qualities work together (the product is easy to use, looks nice, and lasts a long time)

Products' *service* distinctions include:

- **Ordering ease**—how easy it is for customers to buy the product

- **Delivery**—how quickly and accurately the product is delivered

- **Installation**—how well the work is done to make the product usable in its intended location

- **Customer training**—whether your company offers to train customers in using the product

- **Customer consulting**—whether your company offers advice or research services to buyers of the product

- **Maintenance and repair**—how well your company helps customers keep the product in good working order

Positioning and branding your offering

Positioning and branding can constitute additional elements of your marketing strategy. The term *positioning* means determining the *central* benefit of the product and communicating it to the target buyers. For example, a car manufacturer might target buyers for whom safety is a major concern. The company "positions" its cars as the safest vehicles that customers can buy.

Meanwhile, a product *brand* is a name, term, sign, symbol, or design—or any combination of these—that identifies the offering and differentiates it from those of competitors. A well-executed brand creates a strong *brand image*—consumers' perception of what the product or company stands for.

In customers' minds, brands can have meanings that take many different forms. For example, brands can evoke:

- **Attributes.** "This car is durable."

- **Benefits.** "With such a durable car, I won't have to buy another car for years."

- **Values.** "This company certainly emphasizes high performance."

- **Culture.** "I like these cars because they reflect an organized, efficient, high-quality culture."

- **Personality.** "This car really shows off my stylish side."

- **User.** "That looks like the kind of car that a senior executive would buy."

All companies strive to build a clear, favorable brand image for themselves and their products.

Adopting strategies for products

Does your company sell products to its target customers? If so, it's helpful to familiarize yourself with strategies for marketing products. Like human beings, products have life cycles. That is, they're born, and then (over time) their sales grow, mature, and finally decline. The strategies with which you market a product need to change with each of these life-cycle phases.

For example, when a company is introducing a new product to the marketplace, the main goal is to create awareness of the product among consumers and to encourage them to try the new offering. One marketing strategy to achieve these goals is to use heavy promotions.

Once a product starts seeing a growth in sales, the company's marketing objective changes to maximizing market share. Offering product extensions (such as new versions of the product) can help the firm reach this goal.

When a product reaches maturity, the company must shift gears to defending its market share while still maximizing profit. An appropriate marketing strategy at this point in the product's life cycle might be to diversify brands and use promotions to encourage consumers to switch to the new brands.

Finally, most products eventually go into decline. The company's goal becomes seeking to reduce expenditures on a declining product and to "milk" the brand as much as possible. Cutting prices and reducing promotions of the product, as well as phasing out the product entirely, may be appropriate.

Adopting strategies for services

Does your company sell services to its target customers? Designing marketing strategies for services can involve different challenges, because services and products have different characteristics. Compared with products, services are:

- **Intangible.** Customers can't see, touch, smell, or handle services before deciding whether to buy.

- **Inseparable.** Services are usually delivered and consumed simultaneously, so both the provider and the buyer influence the outcome of the service delivery.

- **Variable.** Services vary depending on who provides them and when and where they're provided; thus, controlling their quality is difficult.

- **Transient.** Services are used up on delivery, not stored for future sale.

All these characteristics can make it difficult for customers to judge the quality of a service they've purchased (or are considering purchasing).

So how do you design market strategies that address these unique characteristics of services? Here are some ideas:

- **Select unique processes to deliver your service.** For example, offer self-service instead of table service.

- **Train and motivate employees to serve customers well.**
  This supports the marketing-orientation philosophy that
  "everyone's a marketer!"

- **Develop an attractive physical (or virtual) environment in
  which to deliver the service.** For example, an easy-to-use
  and engaging Web site encourages people to learn about
  your company and buy your service.

- **Differentiate the image associated with your service.** An
  insurance company, for example, might use an image of a
  rock as its corporate symbol to signify strength and stability.

By using your imagination and some creative thinking, you can
design powerful market strategies even for services.

Crafting a Marketing Communications Plan

Executing your marketing strategy calls for an effective marketing communications plan. Marketing communications simply means that you communicate to your target market about the availability, benefits, and price of your company's products or services.

Marketing communications covers the whole range of what most people think of the term *marketing*—advertising, direct sales, sales promotions, public relations, direct marketing, and so on. An effective marketing communications plan has several distinguishing characteristics and can be characterized by "pull" or "push" marketing messages (described later).

Characteristics of an effective plan

Any marketing communication plan will have these defining characteristics:

- The marketing objectives are clearly stated.

- The message matches the target markets' needs or demands.

- Implementation is carefully planned.

- The results are evaluated.

See "Tips for Selecting the Right Marketing Communication Mix" for additional information.

Tips for Selecting the Right Marketing Communication Mix

- Gauge consumer readiness—and adapt your communications tools accordingly.
- Depending on how prepared consumers are to respond to your marketing communications, select the right communication tools for each stage of readiness.
- Tie your choice of communications tools to your product's life-cycle stage. Advertising and publicity, for example, will get you the biggest payoff in the introduction stage of a product.
- Tie your choice of tools to your company rank in the market. Market leaders derive more benefit from advertising than they do from sales promotion. Conversely, smaller competitors gain more by using sales promotion.
- Adapt your communications mix to the product market you're targeting. For example, personal selling can persuade retailers or dealers to buy more stock and display more products, and it boosts dealers' enthusiasm for the product and your company.
- Distinguish between "push" versus "pull" strategies. For example, push strategies can be effective when customers have low brand loyalty, whereas pull strategies are effective when customers have high brand loyalty.

What Would YOU Do?

Crunching the Numbers

GRACE HAS been promoted to brand manager for CrunchPops, a breakfast food offered by the global conglomerate TopFoods, Inc. The cereal is a popular offering with a strong record, but sales have slipped somewhat over the past year.

Grace decides to investigate what's going on in the breakfast cereal market. She also puts some thought into various ways of positioning the product. She knows she needs to prepare a marketing plan to present her ideas. However, she's never prepared one before and is unsure of what to include in the plan. Should she provide an analysis of how CrunchPops compares with TopFoods' overall breakfast cereal line? What about a comparison of all the products that compete with CrunchPops in the breakfast cereal market? Should she share her ideas for exploring consumers' perceptions of CrunchPops and market trends?

The project is starting to seem overwhelming . . .

What would YOU do? The mentors will suggest a solution in *What You COULD Do*.

"Pull" marketing communications

Some marketing communications can be described as "pull." *Pull marketing* is the process of persuading customers to try a product and to continue using the product. *Advertising* is one of the most powerful forms of pull marketing. It is a paid form of impersonal promotion that can appear in many venues:

- Print brochures or flyers

- Billboards

- Point-of-purchase ads

- Television and radio ads

- Web site banners

The strength of pull advertising lies in its ability to:

- **Inform** (give information to the consumer). You use this form of advertising when trying to create awareness of a new product.

- **Persuade** (influence the consumer to buy). You use persuasive ads to focus on competitive advantages of a product.

- **Remind** (maintain consumer awareness). You use reminder ads to keep an aging brand in consumers' minds.

Sales promotions are another form of pull marketing. In this case, you may send out coupons for product savings, contests, free trials, or cash refunds. Companies may choose to use a sales promotion to introduce a new product, build brand loyalty, or gain entry into a new distribution or retail channel.

See "Tips for Creating an Effective Print Ad" and "Tips for Designing a Powerful Sales Promotion" for additional information on developing effective pull-advertising campaigns.

Tips for Creating an Effective Print Ad

- **Clarify the purpose of the ad.** An ad's purpose drives its format and content.

- **Get consumers' attention.** Remember, the average consumer scans an ad in just four seconds. Make your ad as eye-catching as possible.

- **State the product's or service's benefit for consumers.** Your ad should clearly answer the consumer's basic question, "What's in it for me?"

- **Give consumers a reason to act now.** Use language such as "Sale ends Saturday" to create a sense of urgency.

- **Use ad copy to your advantage.** The best copy has a conversational tone, appeals to consumers' interests or concerns, and is short, positive, clear, and complete.

- **Use design to your advantage.** The best designs are fresh, appealing, uncomplicated, uncluttered, and practical. The ad's look and feel should support and enhance the brand image and message.

- **Follow type-treatment guidelines.** Avoid using too many different type sizes and styles.

Tips for Designing a Powerful Sales Promotion

- **Use sales promotions *with* advertising.** For example, combine a price promotion with an ad emphasizing the product's features or with a point-of-purchase display. Or if you're marketing to businesses through trade shows or conventions, combine poster ads with sales-rep selling contests to get the most impact.

- **Be clear about your objectives.** Your goals for sales promotions will vary with your target market. If you're targeting retailers, persuade them to carry your company's new offerings, to stock more inventory, to encourage off-season buying, or to offset competitive promotions.

- **Choose the appropriate promotion tools.** Depending on your objectives, select the right tools. For salespeople, launch sales contests with prizes for the winners. If you're marketing to businesses through trade shows or conventions, use publications, videos, and other audiovisual materials to generate new sales leads, meet new customers face to face, sell more to existing customers, and educate customers.

- **Use sales promotions in markets of high brand *dissimilarity*.** Sales promotions tend to attract brand switchers who look primarily for low price, good value, or premiums. You'll get more—and longer-lasting—market share if you use such incentives in markets of high brand dissimilarity.

- **Distinguish between *price promotions* and *added-value promotions*.** Sales promotions, with their incessant prices off, coupons, deals, and premiums, can devalue the product offering in consumers' minds. Make sure your promotions enhance your brand image.

- **Pretest your sales promotion program.** Use pretests (small trial runs) to determine whether the promotional tools you've chosen are appropriate, the incentive size will produce enough sales response without costing the company too much, and the presentation is efficient.

"Push" marketing communications

Other marketing communications are considered "push." *Push marketing* occurs when the product is presented assertively to the customer by the seller. The most common type of push marketing is when a company uses a direct sales force to call on prospective companies or consumers. It is the salesperson's task to persuade the potential customer to purchase the product.

Salespeople are most effective for the following push marketing tasks:

- Looking for new prospects (people from whom a marketer is seeking a response—whether it's attention, a purchase, or a vote).

- Communicating face-to-face, so that a potential customer's questions and concerns can be directly addressed.

- Selling, which consists of knocking on doors, presenting the product or service, and selling it.

- Servicing, which entails providing services for customers such as repairing or replacing parts for a product.

- Performing market research.

See "Tips for Evaluating Sales Representatives" for additional information on how to get the most "push" value from a sales force.

Tips for Evaluating Sales Representatives

- **Analyze salespeople's annual territory marketing plans.** This report puts sales reps into the role of marketing managers and profit centers. Managers can study these plans, make suggestions, and use the plans to develop sales quotas.

- **Review other reporting documents from sales reps.** Reports on such items as sales calls, expenses, new business, and lost business can be used as raw data, from which you can extract key indicators of sales performance.

- **Compare sales reps' current performance with their past performance and company averages.**

- **Assess performance along more subjective dimensions.** For example, take stock of a sales rep's knowledge of the firm, products, customers, competitors, territory, and responsibilities.

- **Gauge sales reps' professionalism.** Determine whether a sales rep has a customer-oriented approach. Does he or she maintain a professional connection with the customer even after a sale?

- **Assess negotiation skills.** Effective salespeople need to work with customers to reach agreement on price and other terms of sales without making concessions that will hurt your company's profitability.

- **Assess ability to build long-term relationships with customers.** Effective sales reps demonstrate that their company has the desire and ability to serve a customers' needs in a superior way over the long run.

What You COULD Do.

Remember Grace's uncertainty about how to develop a marketing plan for addressing slowing sales of a key product?

Here's what the mentors suggest:

Grace should definitely come up with and document ideas for exploring consumers' perceptions of CrunchPops and market trends. Conducting market research will help her understand customers' perceptions and needs—the first step in the marketing process. Customers' needs drive their purchasing decisions. Successful companies stay informed about changes in those needs and adapt their offerings and product strategies accordingly.

Grace should document her ideas in the market-research section of her marketing plan. The section should contain any prior market research, along with the new research Grace plans to conduct. Marketing plans contain many components in addition to research, such as past and projected performance of the product, the product's unique selling points, a competitive analysis, a target customer profile, and descriptions of intended marketing tactics.

Though it's also important to include information about competitors in a marketing plan, Grace's competitive analysis should focus only on key competitors, their market share, and their specific offerings and prices. Providing details on *all* competing products would make the marketing plan overly lengthy and thus less useful.

Finally, since Grace's job is to manage the CrunchPops brand, she should make sure her marketing plan focuses on that single product—not how the product compares with TopFoods' entire product lineup.

New Offerings: A Potent Marketing Tool

In most businesses, companies are under constant pressure to come up with either entirely fresh offerings or improvements on existing products. Yet new offerings fail at an astounding rate. In fact, 80 percent of recently launched products are no longer around! New products and services fail for many reasons; for example, development costs may prove higher than a company expected, or competitors fight back more fiercely.

What's the best way to make *your* new or improved product or service as successful as possible? Understand the advantages of providing new offerings. Generate and test good ideas. Then develop effective marketing programs for the most promising ones.

The advantages of providing new products and services

Customers (whether they're consumers or organizations) like to have new choices. And successful companies constantly research and create fresh offerings to satisfy these desires and to build sales. But continually coming up with new products or services is important for other reasons as well:

- Customers are often fickle creatures; their attitudes toward existing products or services can change quickly and unexpectedly.

- Most products and services have a natural life cycle and eventually become outdated.

- Your competitors are also looking for ways to offer bigger and better deals to customers.

Generating ideas for new offerings

Start generating new product ideas by asking customers what they need and want or what they're unhappy about. For example, a kitchen supplies company discovered that customers using the company's scrubbing pads didn't like the fact that the pads scratched their expensive cookware. The company acted on this new knowledge—and developed a no-scratch soap pad.

Good ideas don't *always* come from customers. Consumers may not be aware of the available product or service possibilities, or they may not know how to articulate their needs or concerns. Still, any product or service idea will succeed only if it ultimately solves a customer's problem, fulfills a need, or meets approval.

Other sources of new ideas include:

- Your competitors

- Your company's own employees

- Industry consultants and publications

- Market-research firms

Consider using all these resources, in addition to customer feedback, to brainstorm as many ideas as possible.

Evaluating your ideas

Once you've generated ideas for new offerings, determine whether the ideas are compatible with your company's overall strategies and resources. Screen out any ideas that don't fit these criteria. For example, if your firm specializes in expensive office furniture, ask how strongly an idea for a new desk chair might support this strategy. And decide whether the company can afford to develop and launch such a product.

If your new product or service ideas fit with your company's strategic plan, then test the ideas by presenting the concepts to target consumers—perhaps in focus groups or through mail-in questionnaires—and get their reactions. Depending on the product or service, you can create a physical model, or prototype, to show consumers. Or, you can use computer-aided design and manufacturing software to demonstrate the idea.

Testing your ideas in the consumer market

Once you've decided on a new product, the next step is to test it in the market. Test marketing lets you gauge whether the product or service is technically and commercially sound and how enthusiastically target customers may embrace the offering. You can test-market both consumer *and* business goods and services.

To test *consumer offerings*, you can use one or more of the methods listed next. They range from least to most costly. Your firm can hire companies that specialize in conducting and evaluating any or all of these tests.

First, develop samples of the actual offering. You'll want to dress these samples up with a brand name and packaging and then test them in authentic settings, with flesh-and-blood customers. Consider these test tactics:

- **Sales wave.** Let some consumers try the product at no cost. Then reoffer the product, or a competitor's product, at slightly reduced prices. See how many customers choose your product again and gauge their satisfaction with it.

- **Simulated test marketing.** Ask a number of qualified buyers to answer questions about their product preferences. Then invite them to look at a series of commercials or print ads that include one for your new product. Finally, give them some money and set them loose in a store. See how many of them buy your product.

- **Controlled test marketing.** Place your product in a number of stores and geographic locations that you're interested in testing. Test different shelf positions, displays, and pricing. Measure sales through electronic inventory control systems.

- **Test market.** This is test marketing on a grand scale. Select a few representative cities, have your sales force give the product thorough exposure in those cities, and unleash a full advertising and promotion campaign. See how well the product sells.

Testing your ideas in the organizational market

To test *business offerings*, use these methods:

- **Alpha testing.** Build a few units of the new product or create a test pilot for a new service. Then carefully select a couple of your most important and friendliest customers to try the offering for free and comment on its functionality, features, and problems. You might make sure that a representative from your firm visits the alpha-testing customer and "walks" him or her through the testing process. Your goal at this point is to collect advice for making the product or service the best it can be.

- **Beta testing.** This resembles alpha testing, except that it's done a bit later in the product-development process—when the product or service is somewhat closer to its final form. With beta testing, send more units out to more customers for their feedback than you did with alpha testing. You might have a more specific list of concerns or issues that you want testers to think about as they use and experiment with the product or service. And, you might actually offer to sell testers the product at a big discount.

- **Trade-show exhibits.** Observe how much interest participants show in the product or service, how they react to various features, and how many express clear intention of buying the offering or placing an order for it. Note, though, that your competitors will also get a look at your product or service at trade shows. Therefore, it's best to launch the offering soon after the show.

Putting Your
Marketing Plan
into Action

Once you've selected an idea for a promising new offering, you need to develop a marketing plan for it. The marketing plan lays out a campaign that will transform the *product or service concept* into a successful offering that meets target customers' needs.

You can help put your marketing plan into action first by understanding how your company manages its marketing efforts. Then you can more effectively figure out where *you* stand within that structure and determine how you might best work with supervisors, peers, and direct reports to contribute to the marketing plan's implementation.

Managing marketing entails (1) organizing a firm's marketing resources to implement and control the marketing plan, and (2) putting feedback and control structures in place to ensure the plan's success and to respond to any surprises or disappointments.

Understanding how your marketing department works

Marketing departments may be organized on the basis of one of several different emphases. Here are some examples:

- **Function.** Many marketing departments consist of functional specialists—for example, a sales manager and market-research manager who report to a marketing VP. This structure simplifies the administration of marketing, but loses effectiveness if products and markets proliferate. Specifically, products that no one favors may be neglected, and functional groups may compete for budget and status.

- **Geography.** A firm's national sales manager supervises several regional sales managers, who supervise zone managers, who in turn oversee district sales managers, who manage salespeople. Some companies further subdivide regional markets into ethnic and demographic segments and design different ad campaigns for each.

- **Product or brand.** A product or brand manager supervises product-category managers, who supervise specific product and brand managers. This structure works well if the company creates markedly different kinds—or huge numbers—of products. It lets product managers develop a cost-effective marketing mix for each product, respond quickly to marketplace changes, and monitor smaller brands. However, it can result in conflict if product managers don't have enough authority to fulfill their responsibilities.

- **Customer markets.** Companies that sell their products to a diverse set of markets—for instance, offering fax machines to individual consumers, businesses, and government agencies—have a marketing manager who supervises market specialists (sometimes also called industry specialists).

- **Global perspective.** Companies that market internationally may have an export department with a sales manager and a few assistants, or an entire international division with functional specialists and operating units structured geographically, according to product. Or such firms may be truly global organizations—where top managers direct worldwide operations, marketing policies, financial flows, and logistical systems. In these companies, global operating units report directly to top management, not to an international division head.

Developing the right skills

Regardless of how your firm's marketing activities are organized, the company needs to clarify who, where, when, and how different individuals are going to implement a marketing plan. Successful implementation of any marketing plan hinges on these four skill sets:

1. **Diagnosis**—anticipating what might go wrong and preparing for it.

2. **Identification of a problem source**—looking for the source of a problem in the marketing function, the plan itself, the company's policies or culture, or in other areas.

3. **Implementation**—budgeting resources wisely, organizing work effectively, motivating others.

4. **Evaluation**—assessing the results of marketing programs.

Companies staffed by people who have these skills stand an excellent chance of seeing their marketing programs transformed into actual market successes.

Controlling the marketing process

Even when prepared with a cohesive plan, the resources needed, and all the right skills, your company will still encounter surprises while implementing its marketing programs. That's because business—like life—rarely goes exactly according to plan. Here are just a few examples of the many different marketing surprises your firm may experience:

- Customer demand for a product proves lower than your market research led you to believe.

- Consumers use your product in a way you never intended.

- A previously invisible competitor blindsides you with a dazzling new offering.

- The cost of an ad campaign is higher than you estimated.

Constant monitoring and control of the firm's marketing activities can help your company respond effectively to these kinds of unexpected events.

The table "Marketing-Process Controls" shows four types of marketing controls and explains who's responsible, why a company might select this form of control, and how the firm might implement these control measures.

Depending on your role, and your company's choice of control type, you may find yourself responsible for one or more of these activities. Or others in your company may need your help gathering the required information to conduct these assessments.

TABLE 5

Marketing-process controls

Type of control	Who's responsible?	Why this control type?	How to control?
Annual plan	Top and middle managers	To assess whether planned results have been achieved	Analyze sales, market share, marketing expense-to-sales ratio
Profitability	Marketing controllers	To see where the company is making and losing money	Measure profitability by product, territory, customer, segment, channel, order size; measure ROI
Efficiency	Line and staff managers, marketing controllers	To improve the spending and impact of marketing dollars	Measure efficiency of sales force, advertisements, sales promotions, distribution
Strategy	Top managers, marketing auditors	To ask whether the company is pursuing the best market, product, and channel opportunities	Review marketing effectiveness and company's social and ethical responsibilities

Whichever part of the control process you're involved in, you can feel proud about contributing to a key stage in your firm's marketing process.

Spotlight on Direct Marketing

Will you order this year's holiday gifts from catalogs instead of heading for the shopping malls? Have you sent money in response to a mailed-in request for donations to a charitable cause? Has your company been purchasing raw materials over a Web site rather than placing orders with your suppliers' sales force?

If you answered yes to any of these questions, then you've participated in or seen direct marketing in action. Direct marketing is such a specific approach that we've given it a special section in this guide. In the following pages, you'll learn more about what direct marketing is, why it can be useful, what its challenges are, and what channels it uses.

What is direct marketing?

Companies engage in *direct marketing* when they sell their products and services directly to customers *without* the use of intermediaries such as wholesalers, retailers, and so forth. To do so, they can use traditional media, such as printed, mailed marketing pieces; radio or TV spots; telemarketing campaigns; and faxes. They can also use newer media, such as e-mail, Web sites, and online services.

As you may have guessed from the printed marketing materials you receive in your mailbox, or the e-mails you receive at your business or your home, direct marketing is showing remarkable growth.

Why use direct marketing?

Direct marketing has been growing so fast because it provides increased benefits in today's business world of intensifying competition. It enables companies to:

- Buy mailing lists containing the names and contact information of almost any group of target customers, for example, left-handed people, millionaires, or new consulting companies.

- Personalize and customize the messages they deliver to target customers.

- Time the delivery of messages so they reach prospects at the right moment.

- Achieve higher readership of printed materials.

- Test messages and media to find the most cost-effective approach.

- Conceal offerings and strategies from competitors.

- Measure customer responses to identify the most profitable campaigns.

- Integrate direct-marketing strategies with other strategies, such as paid advertisements.

- Reach customers less expensively than through a sales force.

Direct marketing's most important benefit for companies is that it lets firms engage in *relationship marketing*, or *one-to-one marketing.* Through this special kind of marketing, companies build stronger, more profitable bonds with target customers.

How direct marketing benefits customers

Customers—whether individual consumers or businesses—also appreciate direct marketing for many different reasons. Through this type of marketing, they can:

- Shop more easily and quickly from home or office.

- Choose from a larger selection of merchandise.

- Compare products, services, and prices easily.

- Order goods twenty-four hours a day.

- Learn about available products or services without having to meet with salespeople.

- Receive their purchases quickly through next-day delivery services.

In addition, new technology has made it easy for companies to compile *customer databases*, organized collections of updated, accessible information about individual customers or prospects. Your company's customer database lets it:

- **Identify prospects.** The company may generate sales leads by advertising its product and then build a database from the responses that come in. It can sort through the database to identify the best prospects and then contact them by mail, phone, or other means in an attempt to convert them into customers.

- **Decide which customers should receive a particular offer.** The firm defines the ideal target customer for an offer and then searches the database for those customers most closely resembling the ideal.

- **Deepen customer loyalty.** The company can pique customers' interest and enthusiasm by remembering their preferences and sending gifts, coupons, and special information.

- **"Reactivate" customer purchases.** The firm can use automatic mailing programs to send customers birthday or anniversary cards, holiday shopping reminders, or other timely offers.

The dark side of direct marketing

Direct marketing clearly offers crucial benefits to both sellers and buyers. But it also has its dark side—characteristics that might turn customers away from your product or service:

- **Customer irritation.** Many consumers view direct-marketing solicitations as annoying.

- **Unfairness.** Some unscrupulous direct marketers take advantage of impulsive buyers, for example, by using inflated claims to capture customers with low sales resistance.

- **Outright deception and fraud.** These include false claims about products and performance and questionable gimmicks such as envelopes that resemble government documents, which make recipients feel compelled to open and read the contents.

- **Invasion of privacy.** Critics worry that marketers know too much about customers' lives and may use this knowledge to take advantage. For online marketers, consumers are particularly worried about the security of their credit-card numbers and other personal information.

- **Chaos and clutter.** For online marketers, especially, the Internet makes a staggering amount of information possible. Navigating the Web can be frustrating for consumers; thus, many companies' sites go unnoticed.

These problems, if left untended, will ultimately turn customers away from direct marketing. Companies that realize this and work to address these issues—providing honest and well-designed marketing offers only to those consumers who appreciate being contacted—will ultimately be more successful.

Direct-marketing channels

Direct marketing may involve a number of channels. For example:

- **Face-to-face selling**—including individuals who sell products for direct-sales organizations.

- **Direct mail**—including printed offers, announcements, reminders, or other messages sent directly to a person or business at a particular address; nonprinted items mailed to consumers, such as free videos or audiotapes, CDs, and computer disks; and faxes, e-mail, and voice-mail messages.

- **Catalogs**—pamphlets or books describing the company's merchandise and containing order forms or toll-free ordering numbers.

- **Telemarketing**—phone calls designed to attract new customers, contact existing ones, or take orders.

- **Direct-response TV**—such as home-shopping channels and TV ads that invite viewers to call a toll-free number to get more information or place orders.

- **Kiosks**—machines placed in stores, airports, and other locations that allow customers to place orders.

With so many available channels, companies need a systematic approach to deciding which to use in their direct-marketing campaigns.

Online marketing

Electronic communications of all sorts have shown explosive growth, with Internet traffic doubling every hundred days and millions of Web sites open for business and coming online every day. This new technology has taken several forms:

- **The Internet**—the international web of computer networks that makes global communication instantaneous and decentralized

- **Electronic markets**—individual companies' Web sites that (1) describe a firm's offerings, (2) let buyers search for information and place orders using a credit card, and (3) arrange for delivery of the product physically (to the customer's home or office) or electronically (as in the case of software and music downloaded to the customer's computer)

- **Electronic commerce**—business transactions enacted over a wide variety of platforms, such as use of fax or e-mail, automated teller machines (ATMs), and "smart cards" that facilitate payment (such as for long-distance telephone service)

- **Commercial online services**—companies that offer online information and services such as news, entertainment, shopping advice, chat rooms, and e-mail capabilities to paid subscribers

In addition to understanding the various forms of online marketing, companies must understand the differentiating characteristics of online consumers:

- They tend to be younger, more affluent, and better educated than the general population.

- They comprise an almost equal number of men and women.

- They tend to place great value on information.

- Many of them respond negatively to messages aimed only at selling.

- They like to control the information they receive about products and the conditions under which they receive that information.

- They—not the marketers—give permission to be contacted and control the resulting interactions.

- They're well-informed and discerning shoppers.

Online consumers are very much in control, forcing many companies to rethink time-honored approaches to marketing. In light of these characteristics, how can your company best conduct its online marketing efforts? Here are some options to choose from:

- **Establish an electronic presence.** Buy space on a commercial online service, sell products or services through another company's Web site, or open your own corporate Web site or "microsite" (a small, specialized site for specific occasions or products).

- **Advertise online.** Advertise in special sections offered by commercial online services, in Internet newsgroups set up for commercial purposes, or through banner ads and pop-up windows on other companies' Web sites.

- **Participate in or sponsor Internet interest groups.** These groups encourage the spread of "word of Web" about your products and help you to learn how customers perceive your company and its offerings. Groups come in various forms:

  ○ Forums are discussion groups located on commercial online services. These groups may operate a chat room (for real-time message exchanges), a classified-ad directory, and other resources.

- Newsgroups are the Internet version of forums, limited to people who post and read messages on a specific topic.

- Bulletin boards are specialized online services that center on a specific topic or group.

- Web communities are commercially sponsored Web sites where member companies congregate online and exchange views of common interest.

- Blogs are Web sites on which individuals post opinions about all manner of things, including companies and their products or services. Microblogs (such as Twitter) are also gaining popularity.

- **Send e-mails.** Send electronic newsletters, special product offers, reminders of upcoming promotions, and announcements for special events. Invite people to e-mail your firm with questions, suggestions, and complaints. To avoid being labeled as a "spammer" (a company that sends unsolicited e-mail), consider asking for customers' permission before sending e-mail offers.

Direct marketing through both traditional and new media poses both new opportunities and new challenges for companies. However, one thing is certain: as technology continues to evolve and consumers become ever more technologically savvy, marketers from all sorts of industries will need to constantly examine their strategies and programs in a new light. Those who can adapt to changing conditions and technological advances with fresh thinking will dominate.

See "Tips for Marketing Online" for additional ideas.

Tips for Marketing Online

- **Follow standards for online ads.** If you decide to post an ad on the Internet, request ad requirements from the company that's selling the ad space *before* designing your ad.
- **Use the Web as a direct-response tool.** When designing a direct-response ad for the Web, make it easy for the respondent to reach you—through a click-on button, e-mail, phone, fax, and so on.
- **Look for ad-space bargains.** Consider hiring an ad agency or media-buying shop that can help you in your search.
- **Don't forget to *try* to make a sale through a Web ad.** Give consumers this option.
- **Make your own Web site irresistible.** For example, a site that's easy to use will win out over one that's hard to use.
- **Don't forget basic spelling, punctuation, grammar, and editorial standards.** Sloppiness on this front can annoy visitors and drive them away.

Spotlight on Relationship Marketing

The combination of traditional direct-marketing media, such as mailings, radio spots, kiosks, and so forth; new media, including the Internet and e-mail; and recent database technologies has created a whole new approach to marketing. That approach is called *relationship marketing*, or *one-to-one marketing*. In the pages that follow, we examine this type of marketing more closely.

What is relationship marketing?

Through relationship marketing, firms learn more and more about their target customers, often by compiling powerful databases that keep track of buyers':

- Purchasing behavior and history

- Product preferences

- Concerns or complaints about the company's products or services

- Lifestyles

- Other personal characteristics, such as age, marital status, income level, race, and so forth, that could affect buying decisions

Using that information, companies can tailor their marketing communications to attract and maintain those customers. They can also customize their offerings to constantly meet target customers' changing needs.

Why use relationship marketing?

Relationship marketing lets companies build strong, profitable bonds with their target customers. *Organizations* benefit from these bonds because loyal customers generate greater and greater profits every year that they do business with a particular company. How?

- Loyal customers buy more of the company's offerings, and more often; and they tend to spend increasing amounts of money over time.

- At the same time, the cost associated with serving such customers—including entering them in the company's database, getting to know their preferences, and processing information about them—is spread out over time. Thus, that cost decreases with every purchase from a particular customer.

Consumers also benefit from relationship marketing:

- By creating bonds and accumulating a purchasing history with trusted companies, customers can avoid the time-consuming—and often stressful—process of shopping around for the best deal.

- Because these trusted companies know them, customers may hear about attractive products, services, or special offers that they would not have found out about from less familiar companies. Sometimes, companies may even suggest a product that a customer would not have thought attractive on his or her own. In other words, a company may sense a customer's need and identify ways to satisfy it, even before the customer is aware of that need.

The dark side of relationship marketing

Though relationship marketing has enormous potential, it carries a serious risk as well: the danger of irritating consumers with overly frequent contact or requests for personal information. Consumers may resist marketers' efforts to build one-on-one relationships for several reasons.

They simply don't want to invest time and effort in maintaining relationships with companies. Perhaps they would rather cultivate other kinds of relationships or invest time and energy in other areas of their lives. Or they may be uncertain about what kinds of products, services, or attention they want from marketers.

Moreover, consumers often feel that companies are not "pulling their weight" in these arrangements. That is, some people value such one-to-one relationships but feel that firms are repeatedly asking them for personal information without providing any attractive, personalized services in return.

To understand how consumers perceive and respond to relationship-marketing efforts, consider the table "Consumer Perceptions of Relationship Marketing."

TABLE 6

Consumer perceptions of relationship marketing

Consumer perception	Example	Result
"Too many companies want personal relationships with me!"	One consumer receives five mailings in a single day requesting personal information about him or her and promises of valuable offers if he or she responds.	Marketing advances seem trivial, useless, or annoying. Consumers' interest in relationship building evaporates.
"Companies want my friendship, loyalty, and respect—but they're not giving me those same things in return!"	A hotel requests personal information from guests—their address, the purpose of their travels, the number of times they travel each year—but doesn't provide anything in return.	Consumers see marketing as a "one-way street" that benefits companies only.
"Companies treat their best customers like kings and queens—and ignore the rest of their customers!"	A rental-car company drops off "club" members at their cars but makes non-club—but loyal—customers walk.	Loyal customers feel devalued.
"Companies offer too many options—I can't keep them straight in my mind!"	A health-and-beauty-products manutacturer offers a single toothpaste brand in 55 different product and packaging variations.	Customers feel overwhelmed and paralyzed.

Maintaining customer trust while using relationship marketing

To keep consumers' trust in marketers, you can prove—through your actions—that a one-to-one relationship can be valuable and stress-free for customers. To do this, rethink these aspects of marketing:

- **Product design.** Ask whether your new products fulfill customer needs—or just cause confusion or annoyance. Evaluate consumers' likely reactions and then eliminate features or functions that threaten to prove overwhelming or irritating for buyers. For example, one health-and-beauty-products manufacturer has standardized its products' packaging and pruned marginal brands that attracted mediocre consumer attention.

- **Consumer control.** Offer customers tools or methods for controlling the degree of frustration they may encounter in using your products or services. For instance, one Internet service provider's software lets customers block unsolicited e-mails.

- **Handling of personal information.** If your firm is not using the personal information it is gathering from customers, stop collecting it "just in case." Be honest with consumers, too, about why you request personal information: you want to win their business and loyalty. Then, make sure they understand why your deal is the best.

In addition, get to know your company's customers. For example, get as many people as possible—your company's product managers, engineers, package designers, and so on—to visit and talk face-to-face with actual consumers in *their* world. Don't assume that conducting market research within the confines of your office or inviting customers to come talk with you on your company's turf is enough to get to know your customers.

Also, find out how people actually use—and feel about—your company's offerings. You can get an "up-close-and-personal" view of "a day in the life of a customer" through videotape sessions and by photographing customers as they're using your products—all with your customers' permission, of course. You can also invite customers to participate in product-discussion groups on your company's Web site, though if you do so, consider offering them something in return.

By getting to know your customers—and using that knowledge to *genuinely* keep their best interests in mind—you can do your part to achieve a marriage (or at least a relationship) made in heaven.

Tips and Tools

Tools for
Understanding
Marketing

Worksheet for Calculating the Lifetime Value of a Customer

Use this worksheet to calculate the lifetime value of one of your customers.

Customer name:

Basic formula

Estimated # of customer transactions in lifetime		Number of purchases per visit		Average price per purchase ($)		Cost to acquire a customer ($)		Lifetime value of a customer ($)
[ ]	×	[ ]	×	[ ]	−	[ ]	=	[ ]

Projected formula, 5-year period

	Revenue *(Include gross revenue generated)*		Cost *(Calculate costs to service this customer, including marketing and costs of making and delivering product or service)*		Referrals *(Add net value of referred accounts)*		Profit ($)
Year 1	[ ]	−	[ ]	+	[ ]	=	[ ]
Year 2	[ ]	−	[ ]	+	[ ]	=	[ ]
Year 3	[ ]	−	[ ]	+	[ ]	=	[ ]
Year 4	[ ]	−	[ ]	+	[ ]	=	[ ]
Year 5	[ ]	−	[ ]	+	[ ]	=	[ ]
						Total:	

Customer Value Equation Worksheet

Use this worksheet to think through what your customers value, which you can think of as an equation. The service value as determined by the customer is equal to the results received times how the service is delivered, in relation to the price of the service times any costs for acquiring the service. The values in the equation are relative, since different customers often want different things, or the same customer may want different things at different times. For example, your customers may value convenience and the opportunity to save time more in one situation, or price in another. Think through how you can leverage the factors in this equation to add value to the customer and enhance your business.

What Customers Value: *Fill in this equation with descriptions of what your customers value. You do not have to use a specific dollar amount in the price category, but you could use descriptive terms such as high, low, competitive pricing, every day low-price (EDLP), premium, discounted, and so forth.*

Results		**Delivery/process quality**
What results do your customers want?		*How do they want the results delivered?*
	×	

Look at the above in relationship to the factors below.

Price		**Access costs**
What price are they willing to pay for the product or service?		*What costs are they willing to incur to get the product or service?*
	×	

Value summary

What are the key customer value equations most prevalent in your business?

What factors or situations could affect these equations? Which ones can you alter or control?

How can you leverage these factors to increase the value of your service (or product) to the customer? *For example, increase convenience, while keeping price the same.*

Worksheet for Conducting a SWOT Analysis

Use a SWOT analysis to identify the strengths, weaknesses, opportunities, or threats relative to a product, product line, marketing program, or even a whole company. The SWOT analysis lets you focus on specific areas and discover actions that can help build on strengths, minimize or eliminate weaknesses, maximize opportunities, and deal with or overcome threats.

Date of Analysis: _____

Name of Item to Be Analyzed: _____

For example, the Fall Back-to-School Marketing Program.

Internal Analysis

List items inherent to the item to be analyzed, such as positive results of a marketing program.

Strengths	Ideas for building on these strengths
Weaknesses	Ideas for minimizing or strengthening these weaknesses

External Analysis

List items or factors outside of the item to be analyzed, such as external marketplace factors.

Opportunities	Ideas for investigating or taking advantage of these opportunities
Threats	Ideas for minimizing or overcoming these threats

Product Profile Worksheet

Use this form to capture essential planning and control information on a product. You can adapt categories to fit a service or program offering.

Product name:		Date of launch:	
Product number:		Current version:	
Product manager:		Product line:	

Phase in product life cycle: (*Check the one that applies most closely.*)

☐ New product ☐ Growth phase ☐ Mature phase ☐ Decline phase

Manufacturing, assembly, or development site

Product positioning

Target market(s) or segments

Key product features	Key product benefits
1.	1.
2.	2.
3.	3.

Unique selling point

Pricing strategy (*Consider cost, competition, customers' demand, and perceived value.*)

☐ Penetration ☐ Premium ☐ Going rate in marketplace ☐ Other

☐ Cost plus ☐ Target-return ☐ Promotional

☐ Perceived value ☐ Value ☐ Markup

Cost per unit:		Average selling price per unit:	
Break-even point:		Target margin:	

Key competitors	Average selling price	Marketing strategy
1.		
2.		
3.		
4.		
5.		

Market demand for product

Distribution channel	Projected annual dollar revenue	% of total revenue	Year-to-date revenue	% change

Current market share:	Last year: % increase or decrease:

Marketing objective

Promotional strategy

Media plan:

Ad agency name:	Contact information:	
Account executive:		

Publicity strategy:

Publicity manager:	Contact information:	

Up-sell/cross-sell opportunities:

Special offers:

Form for Drafting a Marketing Plan

This form is an abbreviated version of a marketing plan that you can add to or adapt to fit your needs.

Product name: _____

Date of plan: _____   Fiscal year: _____

Marketing manager(s): _____   Contact information: _____

_____

Contributors to the plan: _____   Contact information: _____

_____

Approved by: _____   Approval date: _____

Market review

List key market factors
(*Describe the market in terms of size, growth, segments, geographic factors, and so forth.*)

Describe the industry climate/significant new trends
(*For example, what is the current economic condition of this industry? What new trends are emerging?*)

Competitive environment

	Key competitors	Market share	Offering/price
1.			
2.			
3.			
4.			

The product

Prior year revenue, actual versus forecast

This year revenue forecast (*by distribution channel, if indicated*)

Product status

☐ New product? ☐ Enhanced product? Launch date: _____

	Features	Benefits
1.		
2.		
3.		
4.		
5.		

Product positioning (*Note if prior positioning was effective or needs to be reconsidered.*)

Product differentiator, unique selling point, or competitive advantage

The customer

Relevant customer or user demographics
(*What is the typical user profile[s]? Where are they located and how do you reach them?*)

Buyer behavior (*Why do people buy your product? What needs does it meet? Is it a planned or impulse purchase? How does price figure into their purchase?*)

Distribution channels

Market research plan or usability testing

	What	When	Result
Prior			
Planned			

Opportunity analysis (*See also the SWOT tool.*)

Based on an analysis of the product or service's inherent strengths, weaknesses, external opportunities, and threats, what are the major opportunities and issues facing the product and/or brand?

Financial objectives

Marketing objectives

Marketing strategy

Marketing tactics or action programs

Program	Scheduled dates(s)	Estimated cost
Advertising/media		
Merchandising		
Publicity		
Trade shows/exhibits		
Web marketing		
Promotions		
Endorsements		
Sales incentives		
Sales support materials		
Dealer incentives or terms		
Special offers		
Up sell/cross sell		
Pricing strategy		
Others		

Measures of success (*Specify the expected results that signal success; for example, a 3% click through rate on an e-mail campaign.*)

Projected profit and loss (*See also the Pro Forma tool in Harvard ManageMentor Finance Essentials topic.*)

Revenues	Costs	Margin

Controls (*For example, when will progress toward goals be reviewed and by whom? Is there a contingency plan if actual results deviate from projections?*)

Test Yourself

This section offers ten multiple-choice questions to help you identify your baseline knowledge of marketing. Answers to the questions are given at the end of the test.

1. Marketing is:

   a. The process of comparing competitors' offerings against your own company's products and services, defining your offerings' unique characteristics, and communicating those characteristics to customers through compelling advertisements.

   b. The process of planning and executing the conception, pricing, promotion, and distribution of ideas, goods, and services to create exchanges that satisfy individuals' and a company's goals.

   c. The process of identifying and designing cutting-edge product features that will keep your company's offerings ahead of competitors', testing the features' functionality to ensure reliability, and constantly updating product lines to incorporate the best new features.

2. Which of the following best defines a marketing orientation?

   a. Everyone in the organization is constantly thinking about what the company's customers want and how the firm can satisfy those desires better than its rivals can, in ways that generate the company's desired financial returns.

b. All the members of a firm's marketing department stay as current as possible on the latest marketing theory and technologies through frequent in-house or off-site training, coaching by marketing consultants, and other educational opportunities.

c. Based on the assumption that consumers favor products and services that offer the most quality, performance, or innovative features, companies focus their efforts on constantly designing and improving superior offerings.

3. To analyze marketing opportunities, which two questions should your firm ask first?

a. Who are our potential customers? And how much discretionary income are they willing to spend on our offerings?

b. What are our best-selling products? And how can we improve them so as to attract new customers?

c. Who are our target customers? And why should they buy our product instead of our competitors'?

4. As advances in communications connect sellers and buyers as never before, consumers are finding it easier to compare prices. That makes setting prices increasingly complicated for marketers. Which of the following constitutes an example of an effective pricing strategy?

a. Peg price to your firm's costs rather than target revenues.

b. Revise price often enough to capitalize on market changes.

c. Charge the same price for all market segments to avoid customer complaints.

5. Why should your firm continually generate new products and services or improvements to existing offerings?

a. Consumer attitudes toward existing products can change quickly and unexpectedly, most products eventually become outdated, and your competitors are always looking for ways to offer more attractive deals to customers.

b. Over time, older, established products and services become increasingly more expensive to market and (in the case of products) to manufacture. In addition, the cost of servicing customers who have purchased existing products rises.

c. Product and service design technologies are constantly advancing. If your firm doesn't take advantage of these changes by generating new offerings, your most sophisticated customers may view you as behind the times.

6. Which of the following are *not* potential elements of a brand?

a. A name or term.

b. A symbol or design.

c. A list of product ingredients.

7. Direct marketing means:

a. Presenting your products or services to customers through agents or representatives who demonstrate your offerings in customers' homes or offices.

b. Selling your products or services to customers without the use of intermediaries such as wholesalers, retailers, or agents.

c. Observing customers as they use actual products or services in realistic settings during everyday routines.

8. Relationship marketing means:

a. Learning about customers' purchasing behavior, preferences, concerns and complaints, lifestyles, and demographic characteristics, and then customizing your offerings to meet these customers' changing needs.

b. Using market research to discover your customers' thoughts about how your multiple product lines relate to one another, that is, how the different lines compare and contrast in terms of consumer benefits, pricing, and other characteristics.

c. Building mutually beneficial relationships with new customers by offering them special discounts or sales promotions, as well as giving them opportunities to evaluate and buy new products before other customers can do so.

9. Which of the following is *not* an illustration of the benefits of relationship marketing?

a. Owing to the customer loyalty that relationship marketing lets you build, customers generate greater profits every year because they buy more, and they tend to spend increasing amounts of money over time.

b. Relationship marketing lets your company predict precisely when any customer will defect to one of your competitors.

Thus, you can use that information to design sales promotions and other appeals aimed at retaining such customers.

c. The costs associated with serving the loyal target customers you acquire through relationship marketing are spread out over time. Thus, those costs decrease with every purchase each customer makes.

10. Which of the following best describes a product's life cycle?

a. Product introduction, rising sales and profits, and plateauing sales and profits when competition increases.

b. Product introduction, repeated rising and falling of product sales and profits, and plateauing of sales and profits when the market is saturated.

c. Product introduction, rising sales and profits, peaking sales and profits, and decline of sales and profits.

Answers to test questions

1, b. All marketing efforts need to include decisions about products (which include ideas, goods, and services), price, promotion, and place (distribution). Moreover, successful marketing efforts take into account both consumers' and the company's goals. Finally, marketing consists of both planning and implementation.

2, a. A true marketing orientation means that all employees in an organization consider marketing part of their job. Whether they're working at the executive, front-line, or administrative levels, in the accounting department, on the shop floor, or in human resources, all employees can learn how their daily actions affect the firm's ability to meet customers' needs effectively. Armed with this knowledge, they can continually identify and leverage opportunities to help the company better meet those needs.

3, c. By identifying your target customers (the individual consumers or organizations that would most benefit from your firm's products or services) and your offerings' advantages over your competitors', you can design more focused, effective marketing programs. These programs will enable you to communicate your products' key benefits specifically to those people or organizations most likely to be interested in them.

4, b. Of all four marketing-mix elements (product, price, place, and promotion), price is the easiest to change. And experts recommend revising price often to capitalize on market changes. Additional effective pricing strategies include pegging price to your firm's desired revenues rather than its costs, integrating your pricing strategy with the other three Ps, and varying price enough to accommodate different products, market segments, and purchase situations.

5, a. The need to constantly generate new offerings stems from three sources: changing consumer attitudes, the nature of product life cycles, and the actions of your competitors.

6, c. Brands may consist of a name, term, sign, symbol, design— or any combination of these—that instantly identifies your firm's offering and differentiates it from those of competitors. Thus, a list of product ingredients does not constitute a potential element of a brand. A well-executed brand creates a strong brand image or consumer perception of what your product or company stands for. In customers' minds, a brand's meaning can take many different forms, for example, attributes ("This car is durable"), benefits ("With such a durable car, I won't have to buy another car for years"), values ("This company certainly emphasizes high performance"), and personality ("This car really shows off my stylish side").

7, b. You can engage in direct marketing through traditional means (such as printed, mailed marketing pieces; radio or TV broadcasts; telemarketing; and faxes) or through newer media (such as e-mail, the Internet, and online marketing services). But regardless of which media you use, direct marketing means selling to customers without the use of intermediaries.

8, a. At its heart, relationship marketing entails getting to know the individual consumers who make up narrower and narrower market segments, and then shaping your products and services to meet those customers' specific and changing needs.

9, b. The ability to predict precisely when a customer will defect to a competitor is actually *not* something you gain through relationship marketing. Rather, relationship marketing lets you create close, loyal bonds with target customers. Loyal customers become more profitable because they buy more from you, spending increasing amounts each time. At the same time, the costs of serving them (entering them in your database, learning their preferences) are spread out over time, thereby decreasing with every purchase a customer makes. The key benefit to relationship marketing is thus customer longevity.

10, c. These four phases of the product life cycle are also known as product introduction, growth, maturity, and decline. During the introduction phase, the product generates low sales and profits, thus attracting few competitors. During the growth phase, sales and profits rise, attracting more and more competitors. During the maturity phase, sales and profits peak, and the number of competitors remains stable or declines. And during decline, sales and profits decrease, along with the number of competitors.

Key Terms

Advertising. Any paid form of nonpersonal presentation and promotion of ideas, goods, or services by an identified sponsor.

Brand. A company or product name, term, sign, symbol, design—or combination of these—that identifies the offerings of one company and differentiates them from those of competitors.

Brand image. A customer's perceptions of what a brand stands for. All companies strive to build a strong, favorable brand image.

Competition. All of the actual and potential rival offerings and substitutes that a buyer might consider.

Competitor. Any company that satisfies the same customer needs that another firm satisfies.

Demand. A want for a specific product that is backed by a customer's ability to pay. For example, you might *want* a specific model car, but your want becomes a *demand* only if you're willing and able to pay for it.

Differentiation. The act of designing a set of meaningful differences to distinguish a company's offering from competitors' offerings.

Exchange. The core of marketing, exchange entails obtaining something from someone else by offering something in return.

Industry. A group of firms that offer a product or class of products that are close substitutes for each other.

Marketer. Someone who is seeking a response—attention, a purchase, a vote, a donation—from another party.

Marketing. The process of planning and executing the conception, pricing, promotion, and distribution of ideas, goods, and services to create exchanges that satisfy individual and organizational goals.

Marketing channels. Intermediary companies between producers and final consumers that make products or services available to consumers. Also called *trade channels* or *distribution channels*.

Marketing concept. The belief that a company can achieve its goals primarily by being more effective than its competitors at creating, delivering, and communicating value to its target markets. The marketing concept rests on four pillars: (1) identifying a *target market*, (2) focusing on *customer needs*, (3) coordinating all marketing functions from the *customer's point of view*, and (4) achieving *profitability*.

Marketing mix. The set of tools—product, price, place, and promotion—that a company uses to pursue its marketing objectives in the target market.

Marketing network. A web of connections among a company and its supporting stakeholders—customers, employees, suppliers, distributors, and others—with whom it has built profitable business relationships. Today, companies that have the best marketing networks also have a major competitive edge.

Market-oriented strategic planning. The managerial process of developing and maintaining a viable fit among a company's objectives, skills, and resources and its changing market opportunities.

Need. A basic human requirement, such as food, air, water, clothing, and shelter, as well as recreation, education, and entertainment.

Positioning. The central benefit of a market offering in the minds of target buyers. For example, a car manufacturer that targets buyers for whom safety is a major concern would position its cars as the safest that customers can buy.

Procurement. The process by which a business buys materials or services from another business, with which it then creates products or services for its own customers.

Product. Any offering that can satisfy a customer's need or want. Products come in ten forms: goods, services, experiences, events, persons, places, properties, organizations, information, and ideas.

Product concept. The belief that consumers favor products that offer the most quality, performance, or innovative features.

Production concept. The belief that customers prefer products that are widely available and inexpensive.

Profitable customer. An individual, household, or company that, over time, generates revenue for a marketer that exceeds, by an acceptable amount, the marketer's costs in attracting, selling to, and servicing that customer.

Prospect. A party from whom a marketer is seeking a response—whether it's attention, a purchase, a vote, or something else.

Pull marketing. A type of marketing that attempts to persuade the customer to try a product and continue to use the product. One of the most common types of pull marketing is advertising.

Push marketing. A type of marketing in which the product is "pushed" from the seller to the consumer. The most common type of push marketing is when a company uses a direct sales force to call on prospective companies or consumers.

Relationship marketing. Building long-term, mutually satisfying relations with key parties—such as customers, suppliers, and distributors—to earn and retain their long-term business.

Sales promotion. A collection of incentive tools, usually short term, designed to stimulate consumers to try a product or service, to buy it quickly, or to purchase more of it.

Satisfaction. A customer's feelings of pleasure or disappointment resulting from comparing a product's perceived performance with the customer's expectations of that performance.

Selling concept. The belief that companies must sell and promote their offerings aggressively because consumers will not buy enough of the offerings on their own.

Societal marketing concept. The belief that a company's task is to identify the needs, wants, and interests of target markets and to deliver the desired satisfactions better than competitors do—but in a way that preserves or enhances consumers' and society's well-being.

Supply chain. The long series of activities that result in the creation of raw materials, then components, and then final products that are carried to final buyers. A supply chain includes the marketing channels that bring products to customers.

Value. The ratio between what a customer gets and what he or she gives in return.

Want. A desire that occurs when a need is directed to specific objects that might satisfy that need; for example, a hamburger is a *want* that might satisfy the *need* for food.

Frequently Asked Questions

Why must my company constantly push itself to generate new products and services? Shouldn't our established offerings be enough if they're high quality and successful?

Unfortunately, no. Though your existing products and services may currently meet customers' needs and generate the financial returns your company is looking for, all that could change more quickly than you might realize. For example, consumer attitudes toward existing products can shift rapidly and unexpectedly. In addition, most products have a natural life cycle and eventually become outdated. Finally, your competitors are always looking for ways to offer more attractive options to customers. Thus, to sustain its success, your firm must continually identify and leverage opportunities either to generate entirely new offerings or to create attractive improvements to existing ones.

What are the *biggest* changes in business that my firm should be aware of in designing its marketing efforts?

The business world is always changing, and different developments have more importance at different times. However, at the dawn of the new century, the toughest market challenges include the following: more global competitors are making high-quality products at lower costs, intense price cutting and discounting in all industries are prompting buyers to "shop" for the lowest prices, technological advances (such as the Internet) are making it easier for consumers to price shop and play companies against each other, more and more distributors are dictating terms to manufacturers, the mass market is splintering into many micromarkets requiring tailored marketing efforts, and market costs are rising owing to the declining effectiveness of mass media and the steep costs of personal selling. Despite these challenges, your company needs to find new opportunities.

Marketing seems to be a huge subject. What's the best way for me to master it quickly?

Marketing *is* a huge subject. Although you can certainly grasp the basics by going through this topic, taking some courses in it, reading books on your own, and talking with marketing specialists in your firm, marketing actually takes time and experience to master. That's because marketing problems don't exhibit the neat, measurable properties that problems in the production, accounting, and finance areas can demonstrate. Psychological forces play a large role in marketing problems, and marketing expenditures affect demand and costs simultaneously. Also, every marketing plan both shapes and is shaped by other business-function plans—confusing matters even further. Thus, marketing decisions often need to be made in the face of insufficient information about processes that are ever shifting, interactive, and unusually complex. All this points to the need for not only patience, but also better strategic theory and sharper analytical tools and a great deal of common sense!

I work for a not-for-profit organization. Am I correct in assuming that our firm doesn't need to engage in marketing with quite the same energy that a for-profit corporation does?

Actually, all organizations—if they hope to achieve their missions and sustain their success—need to adopt a strong marketing orientation. Even though not-for-profit organizations may not be setting out to improve shareholder returns, they still provide some sort of exchange with or service for people. They face the same *kinds* of marketing problems that for-profit corporations must grapple with.

For example, colleges compete for students, museums try to attract visitors, performing-arts organizations work to develop audiences, churches and other spiritual centers seek members—and all of them need funding. Moreover, individuals market themselves: politicians seek votes, doctors seek patients, and artists seek celebrity.

What's common to all of these cases? A desire to attract a *response* or *resource* from someone else—whether it's that person's attention, interest, desire, purchase, or positive word-of-mouth. But to elicit those responses, one must offer something that someone else views as valuable. Thus *exchange* is the core concept underlying all marketing.

What's the latest in marketing theory and practice?

Here's one that comes to mind: with the intensifying interest in relationship marketing, some scholars today are questioning whether the core concept underlying marketing should be *exchange* or *relationship* or *network*. As the forces of technology and globalization continue to grow apace, insights into this question will come into sharper focus. One thing is certain, however: computers and the Internet will continue to catalyze enormous changes in buying and selling behavior.

What big marketing lessons have other companies learned that I should be paying attention to?

Perhaps the biggest lesson has to do with globalization. No longer does one country, industry, or company have an exclusive lead on quality, creativity, or capital. More and more, formerly complacent companies have learned that they can no longer afford to ignore foreign competitors, foreign markets, and foreign sources of supply. Moreover, companies can't allow their wage and material costs to get far out of line with the rest of the world. Nor can they ignore emerging technologies, materials, equipment, and ways of organizing.

Equally important, all too many companies have learned the hard way that they must focus first on customer satisfaction and second on profits; that is, they need to rely first on marketing and second on selling. To be sure, these shifts in perspective require major attitude changes. However, companies must make these changes if they hope to both survive and thrive in the ever-changing world of business.

To Learn More

Articles

Allen, James, Frederick F. Reichheld, and Barney Hamilton. "Tuning In to the Voice of Your Customer." *Harvard Management Update*, October 2005.

A Bain & Co. survey reveals just how commonly companies misread the market. Surveying 362 firms, the company found that 80 percent believed they delivered a "superior experience" to their customers. But when researchers asked customers about their own perceptions, they found that they rated only 8 percent of companies as truly delivering a superior experience. Clearly, it's easy for leading companies to assume they're keeping customers happy; it's quite another thing to achieve that kind of customer devotion. So what sets the elite 8 percent apart? They take a distinctively broad view of the customer experience. Learn how to transform your company into one that is continually led and informed by its customers' voices.

Jones, Thomas O., and W. Earl Sasser. "Why Satisfied Customers Defect." *Harvard Business Review OnPoint Enhanced Edition*. Boston: Harvard Business School Publishing, June 2001.

Most managers rejoice if the majority of customers who respond to customer-satisfaction surveys say they are satisfied.

But some of those managers may have a big problem. When most customers say they're satisfied but not completely satisfied, they're saying that they're unhappy with some aspect of the product or service. If they have the opportunity, they will defect. Companies that excel in satisfying customers excel both in listening to customers and in interpreting what customers with different levels of satisfaction are telling them.

Nunes, Paul F., Brian A. Johnson, and R. Timothy S. Breene. "Selling to the Moneyed Masses." *Harvard Business Review*, July 2004.

Over the past decade, the distribution of household incomes has shifted so much that a much larger proportion of consumers now earns significantly higher-than-average incomes—while still falling short of being truly rich. As a result, what used to be a no man's land for new product introductions has in many categories become an extremely profitable "new middle ground." How can marketers capitalize on this new territory? The key, say the authors, is to rethink the positioning and design of offerings and the ways they can be brought to market.

Pitt, Leyland F., Pierre Berthon, Richard T. Watson, and Michael Ewing. "Pricing Strategy and the Net." *Business Horizons*, March 2001.

The Internet is overturning established assumptions about price. For one thing, it facilitates customers' ability to make rather than take a price, as customers and firms engage in one-on-one negotiation and products become commodities. At the same time, the Internet enables firms to differentiate pricing in an instant, create customer switching barriers, "de-menu" pricing, and reduce transactions costs. The authors propose a way to assess Internet-based pricing dynamics and market forms according to the relative strengths of buyer and seller. Pricing, they argue, may prove the last frontier for marketing creativity.

Seybold, Patricia. "Get Inside the Lives of Your Customers." *Harvard Business Review*, May 2001.

Many companies have become adept at the art of customer-relationship management. They've collected mountains of data on preferences and behavior; divided buyers into ever-finer segments; and refined their products, services, and marketing pitches. But all too often, those efforts are too narrow; they concentrate only on the points where the customer comes into contact with the company. Few businesses have bothered to look at what the author calls the customer scenario—the broad context in which customers select, buy, and use products and services. As a result, they've routinely missed chances to deepen loyalty and expand sales. This article showcases three very different companies—National Semiconductor, Tesco, and Buzzsaw.com—that have successfully used customer scenarios as the centerpiece of their marketing plans.

Yankelovich, Daniel, and David Meer. "Rediscovering Market Segmentation." *Harvard Business Review*, February 2006.

In 1964, Daniel Yankelovich introduced in the pages of *Harvard Business Review* the concept of nondemographic segmentation, by which he meant the classification of consumers according to criteria other than age, residence, income, and such. Today, the technique is used almost exclusively to fulfill the needs of advertising, which it serves mainly by populating commercials with characters viewers can identify with. In this article, Yankelovich and consultant David Meer argue the case for a broad view of nondemographic segmentation. They describe the elements of a smart segmentation strategy, explaining how segmentations meant to strengthen brand identity differ from those capable of telling a company which markets it should enter and what goods to make. And they introduce their "gravity of decision spectrum," a tool that focuses on the form of consumer behavior that should be of the greatest interest to marketers—the importance that consumers place on a product or product category.

Books

Harvard Business School Publishing. *Harvard Business Review on Customer Relationship Management.* Harvard Business Review Paperback Series. Boston: Harvard Business School Press, 2002.

This collection of cutting-edge articles shows you how to strengthen customer loyalty through unique relationship-building strategies such as partnerships, branding, and superlative customer service. Contents include: "Co-opting Customer Competence," by C. K. Prahalad and Venkatram Ramaswamy; "Get Inside the Lives of Your Customers," by Patricia B. Seybold; "The Old Pillars of New Retailing," by Leonard L. Berry; "Want to Perfect Your Company's Service? Use Behavioral Science," by Richard B. Chase and Sriram Dasu; "Don't Homogenize, Synchronize," by Mohanbir Sawhney;

"Firing Up the Front Line," by Jon R. Katzenbach and Jason A. Santamaria; "Preventing the Premature Death of Relationship Marketing," by Susan Fournier, Susan Dobscha, and David Glen Mick; and "See Your Brands Through Your Customers' Eyes," by Chris Lederer and Sam Hill.

Hill, Sam, and Chris Lederer. *The Infinite Asset: Managing Brands to Build New Value.* Boston: Harvard Business School Press, 2001.

More than ever, marketers urgently need tools to manage vast groups of brands—not as individual elements or collections under one corporate roof, but as complex systems that transcend corporate boundaries. *The Infinite Asset* is the first book to provide such a model and a proven tool kit to implement it. The authors use in-depth case studies—3M, Cadillac, PING, and Miller Beer—to illustrate how brands add both economic and strategic value to companies, especially during economic downturns. They discuss how a robust brand system enables a company to create, grow, and replenish its brands regularly for products and services in both consumer and business-to-business markets, and to hedge against ever-present market risks. The book provides marketers with the first strategic approach to resolving tough questions about the role of the brand manager in the twenty-first century.

Kotler, Philip, Dipak C. Jain, and Suvit Maesincee. *Marketing Moves: A New Approach to Profits, Growth, and Renewal.* Boston: Harvard Business School Press, 2002.

The authors dismiss the popular view of marketing as an either/or proposition (traditional versus Internet) and argue for a radically different, holistic view of marketing that encompasses both off- and online worlds. The authors show that the old style of marketing is fast losing its effectiveness. Indeed, many dot-coms failed because they viewed marketing as merely advertising, promotion, and sales activities. To succeed today, marketing must move beyond a sideline function and take a central strategic role instead. It must supply the strategic architecture for the company and its collaborators. To do this, marketing must assume responsibility for four core company processes: creating marketing offerings, configuring marketing activities, designing the value chain, and implementing the company's systems. The new realities of the marketplace require a whole new set of tools and concepts. Thought provoking and comprehensive, *Marketing Moves* provides a practical framework for embedding marketing into the heart of your firm's corporate strategy.

Kumar, Nirmalya. *Marketing as Strategy: Understanding the CEO's Agenda for Driving Growth and Innovation.* Boston: Harvard Business School Press, 2004.

It seems that CEOs are increasingly frustrated by marketing's inability to deliver results. Has the profession lost its relevance? The author argues that, although the function of marketing has lost ground, the importance of marketing as a mind-set—geared toward customer focus and market orientation—has gained momentum across the entire organization. This book challenges marketers to change their role from implementers of traditional marketing functions to strategic coordinators of organizationwide initiatives aimed at profitably delivering value to customers.

Li, Charlene, and Josh Bernoff. *Groundswell: Winning in a World Transformed by Social Technologies.* Boston: Harvard Business Press, 2008.

Corporate executives are struggling with a new trend: people using online social technologies to discuss products and companies, write their own news, and find their own deals. This groundswell is global, it's unstoppable, it affects every industry—and it's utterly foreign to the powerful companies running things now. When consumers you've never met are rating your company's products in public forums with which you have no experience or influence, your company is vulnerable. In *Groundswell*, Charlene Li and Josh Bernoff of Forrester, Inc., explain how to turn this threat into an opportunity. Using tools and data straight from Forrester, you'll learn how to evaluate new social technologies as they emerge, determine how different groups of consumers are participating in social technology arenas, apply a four-step process for formulating your future strategy, and build social technologies into your business. Timely and insightful, this book is required reading for executives seeking to protect and strengthen their company's public image.

McKenna, Regis. *Total Access: Giving Customers What They Want in an Anytime, Anywhere World.* Boston: Harvard Business School Press, 2002.

Dominated by hype, and increasingly automated by technology, marketing is losing control over its very reason for existing: to sustain customer relationships. The irony, says McKenna, is that even as technological advances are driving marketing into obscurity, technology is still marketing's only hope for regaining a prominent place in today's organizations. McKenna sets forth a new marketing paradigm in which machines and networks do most of the work. The obsessive emphasis on brand creation and customer manipulation gives way to a focus on discovering individual customer preferences and integrating the people and tools to deliver them. The end goal? A networked marketing ecosystem aimed at providing a "persistent presence" to customers—anytime, anywhere. To achieve this goal, marketers must become IT-centered systems integrators who engage the entire business in the process of change. They must also embrace a new mind-set in which marketing is everything—and everyone's responsibility. Written by the renowned "father of high-tech marketing," this rousing manifesto redefines success in our networked world.

Other information sources

The following Web sites offer information on business, marketing associations, and international commerce:

Business

Financial news: www.bloomberg.com

Technology: www.cnet.com

Companies: www.hoovers.com

Public companies: www.sec.gov

Industry trends and competition: www.stat-usa.gov

Marketing associations

American Marketing Association: www.MarketingPower.com

CommerceNet: www.commerce.net

Gale's Encyclopedia of Associations: www.gale.com

International business

CIA World Factbook: https://www.cia.gov/library/publications/
the-world-factbook/index.html

Embassy sites: www.embassy.org

Sources for Understanding Marketing

The following sources aided in development of this book:

Best, Roger J. *Market-Based Management: Strategies for Growing Customer Value and Profitability*. 2nd ed. Upper Saddle River, NJ: Prentice-Hall, 2000.

Fournier, Susan, Susan Dobscha, and David Glen Mick. "Preventing the Premature Death of Relationship Marketing." *Harvard Business Review*, January–February 1998.

Harvard Business School Publishing. *Finance Essentials*. Harvard ManageMentor Series. Boston: Harvard Business School Publishing, 2000.

Harvard Business School Publishing. *Focusing on Your Customer*. Harvard ManageMentor Series. Boston: Harvard Business School Publishing, 2000.

Harvard Business School Publishing. *Preparing a Business Plan*. Harvard ManageMentor Series. Boston: Harvard Business School Publishing, 2000.

Kotler, Philip. *A Framework for Marketing Management*. Upper Saddle River, NJ: Prentice-Hall, 2001.

Kotler, Philip. *Marketing Management: Analysis, Planning, Implementation, and Control.* 7th ed. Englewood Cliffs, NJ: Prentice-Hall, 1991.

Polaroid Corporation. *Creating Ads That Sell.* Cambridge, MA: Polaroid Corporation, 1987.

Stevens, Robert, David Loudon, Bruce Wrenn, and William Warren. *Marketing Planning Guide.* 2nd ed. Binghamton, NY: The Haworth Press, 1997.

Wrenn, Bruce. Personal communications to the writer, October 1–30, 2001.

Notes

Notes

Notes

Notes

Notes

Notes

Notes

Notes

Notes

Notes

Notes

Notes

Notes

How to Order

Harvard Business School Press publications are available world-wide from your local bookseller or online retailer.

You can also call:
1-800-668-6780

Our product consultants are available to help you 8:00 a.m.–6:00 p.m., Monday–Friday, Eastern Time. Outside the U.S. and Canada, call: 617-783-7450.

Please call about special discounts for quantities greater than ten.

You can order online at:
www.HBSPress.org